CURIOSITIES of SOMERSET

Lornie Leete-Hodge

BOSSINEY BOOKS

For my mother — Millicent Leete

First published in 1985
by Bossiney Books
St Teath, Bodmin, Cornwall

ISBN 0 906456 98 3

Designed, printed and bound in Great Britain by
A. Wheaton & Co. Ltd, Exeter

About the Author — and the Book

Lornie Leete-Hodge was born and lives in Wiltshire, but has strong links with Somerset through her mother who was born in Weston-super-Mare. An Editor by profession, she is a former Editor of *Wessex Life* and other magazines, and author of a number of books including four on Wiltshire, a local history of her birthplace, two novels, many children's books, a Royal Wedding book and a best-selling biography of *Diana, Princess of Wales*. She was also a contributor to *Strange Somerset Stories*. She loves history, especially English, and when not writing she edits other people's books!

Somerset was once described as a county of three C's — cider, cheese and churches. This is still very true, but in this book the author has added a fourth C in describing some of the county's curiosities. There are many ranging from mysterious caves, follies, barrows, beacons, churches to dovecotes, gorges, inns, moors and museums. New oddities to puzzle the thinkers or merely the curious are still being found, and there is a wealth of the unusual in this lovely, often overlooked county that is the essence of England. It is somewhere in which to search and enquire for the rewards are rich.

Plate Acknowledgments

Front cover by Mark Bygrave
Back cover by Julia Davey
Julia Davey; pages 7, 9, 11–23, 26–32, 34–39, 44–48, 52, 57–59, 62, 65–72, 76–90, 92, 94, 100
Ray Bishop: pages 49, 61, 64, 101
Sharp's Studios: pages 10, 42, 43, 60
Felicity Young: pages 25, 56
Don Richmond: page 33
Pcter Friend: page 51
Rosemary Clinch: page 91
Maps by Paul Honeywill

Contents

Introduction

Westcountry Somerset is a county bordered by land on three sides with the sea on its western edge. To some, its shape resembles that of a medieval shoe with pointed toe and heel, and it is wrapped round by Wiltshire, Dorset and Devon. The boundary where the three counties meet is marked by Egbert's Stone at Bourton which once fell into the River Stour, but was rescued and re-erected. In 878 it formed the rallying point for Alfred's troops, and his grandfather, Egbert, was said to have placed it to settle the shire boundaries.

All too often Somerset is overlooked by people hurrying on to holiday resorts in Devon and Cornwall and they miss a great deal. It has an uniqueness in its air of peace and tranquillity with its so-called fairy islands and green meadows of enchantment. It offers a varied landscape with the hills of the Mendips, Quantocks, Brendons, Polden and Blackdown dipping down into the valleys and rippling streams, so characteristic of the area. The coastline is long but with few ports, and it lacks the ruggedness of nearby Cornwall.

Somerset is one of the few counties which was originally the settlement of a single tribe — the Somersaetas — from whom it takes its name. Thirteen hundred years ago, the Saxons in the west fattened their cattle on the rich pastures, always well watered and fertile, and they called it 'Summer land' — the origin of Somerset.

Always essentially English, it boasts a proud history and the men of Somerset hold their heads high. The green hills of their county are remembered in legend and song and they are proud of their

Right: '. . . others find peace . . . in the beauty of Wells Cathedral.'

inheritance. Of gentler disposition than their Wiltshire neighbours, they have a placidity and calmness and a tolerance for strangers, maybe because of their environment.

There is something about the loneliness and vastness of Exmoor with its beauty and its dangers that will always draw people, while others find infinite peace on Glastonbury Tor or in the beauty of Wells Cathedral. For others, the unexpected offers solace and inspiration — the streams that dapple and splash happily in wooded valleys, the flowers in abundance or the birdsong. The sadness of Sedgemoor, like Flodden Field centuries before, when the flower of Somerset's youth marched out bravely in a lost cause on a summer day three hundred years ago is still evident, and the scars of the terrible retribution exacted remain. It is the intangibility of the county that often attracts, and it offers something for all who come to find.

The fertile lands provide good food in plenty and Somerset is world-known for its cheese — Cheddar, Lymeswold and now Melbury. Apples grow in abundance so cider-making is a major industry, while some make it on farms and call it 'Scrumpy'. Rough cider is called Tanglefoot. A rhyme runs:

Beer on cider makes a good rider
Cider on beer makes you feel queer.

Eels are another delicacy many enjoy.

As Wales is the land of song so Somerset is the land of legend and it is steeped in superstition and folklore. There is the belief that Christ came to Glastonbury with Joseph of Arimathea. The Arthurian legend is fundamental to the county — even the burial places of Arthur and his queen can be seen, with Cadbury a superb Camelot. And in modern times the fiction of *Lorna Doone*, created by R. D. Blackmore, has a heroine to rank alongside Jane Eyre or Cathy in *Wuthering Heights*. So much of Lorna's tale is believable with farms, bogs, Oare Church and even John Ridds in the parish register, that thousands come to look and savour 'her' area each year, and it is a mecca for tourists as Glastonbury is for pilgrims.

Witches were part of the scene with the Witch of Wookey Hole caves frozen into immortality. The witches had special ladders for getting into houses. One was found at Wellington, and consisted of a rope with a loop at one end, and thorns and feathers placed along

Glastonbury Tor. 'There is the belief that Christ came to Glastonbury with Joseph of Arimathea.'

'There is something about the loneliness and vastness of Exmoor (above) . . . that will always draw people. For others the unexpected offers solace and inspiration — the flowers in abundance (right).'

the rest at regular intervals. One 'good' witch called Mother Shipton was associated with Porlock and she predicted the tides. She died in 1561 and her prophecies were popular and printed. Others — as in many counties — were said to change into hares to escape and avoid capture, and often farmers shooting a hare were surprised to find a dead woman in their fields.

Pixies were also common, and an ancient encampment on Worlebury Hill dating from the first century BC has extensive fortifications. Its history is intermingled with that of early Britain, with traces of Iron and Bronze Age occupation. The Romans left

their coins and the Danes sought refuge from Alfred there. And pixies were there in force. Red-clothed fairies were said to have been last seen at Buckland St Mary where they were defeated in a pitched battle with the pixies. Afterwards the land was called Pixyland. The fairies' faint cries for help can be heard by those with good ears — so it is said — and the pixies recognised by their red hair and pointed ears!

A maze of footpaths meets and a loose heap of stones marks the spot at Birnbeck known as Peak Winnard. A local superstition claims that Worlebury fishermen crossing the woods to their nets at

Two facets of the Somerset landscape.
Below: Sheep and sheep dog.
Right: Famous Cheddar Gorge.

Birnbeck add a stone as they pass, chanting casually

Picwinner, Picwinner
Pick me some dinner.

to ensure a good catch.

When building a house it was thought unlucky to use stones from a church and some found ill luck after taking stones from a barrow. It was once the custom to put a dead lizard under the foundations of a field wall to ensure its stability. Excavations at one Exmoor cottage revealed that clay pipes had been placed in the chimney and fireplace, and the hearts of animals, such as bullocks, were often put there as a precaution against evil spirits.

Yews were planted in churchyards and branches placed under

the dead as part of the funeral ceremony, being emblems of resurrection. The Druids used yew to prevent their cattle straying over unfenced burial places.

Animals were also protected by hanging a stone with a natural hole in it in the cowshed wall as such stones were believed to be supernatural.

Cobwebs were often used to stop bleeding. After the Battle of Sedgemoor a badly wounded man was hidden in a church chest by the sexton and his wife. She sat on top, in labour, and the searching soldiers left without finding their quarry. Later, when the man was lifted out, cobwebs had covered his wounds and the bleeding had stopped.

Somerset, apart from its famous Exmoor ponies, also has an ancient and unusual breed of horses known as Merriott Spotted Horses. They are spotted, like leopards, and it is thought they are descended from prehistoric forest ponies, sacred to the tribes. They are friendly, docile, tractable animals which were used for transporting food and supplies to markets and also for racing. In the Yeovil area it was thought unlucky to speak of 'spotted' horses. They had belonged to a pagan religion and the church frowned on them. These days they are a rare but preserved breed.

This green land is rich in customs from Harvest Suppers to Punkie Night at Hinton St George when villagers parade the streets by lantern light. St James's Day on 25 July is marked by the apples in the orchards being 'christened' — another old county saying. But it is on the old Twelfth Night, 17 January, that the apple orchards ring with noise and tradition. 'Wassailing' to ward off evil spirits takes place with toast strung on branches and scrumpy poured over the roots — even shots are fired to keep trouble away —and all presided over by the Wassail Queen.

Somerset is one of England's loveliest counties, offering a feast of interest for those who seek it. Its people are proud but not boastful — they just *know* their county is their pride and, to them, the very best.

Right: The beach at Porlock Weir. 'One good "witch" called Mother Shipton was associated with Porlock and she predicted the tides.'

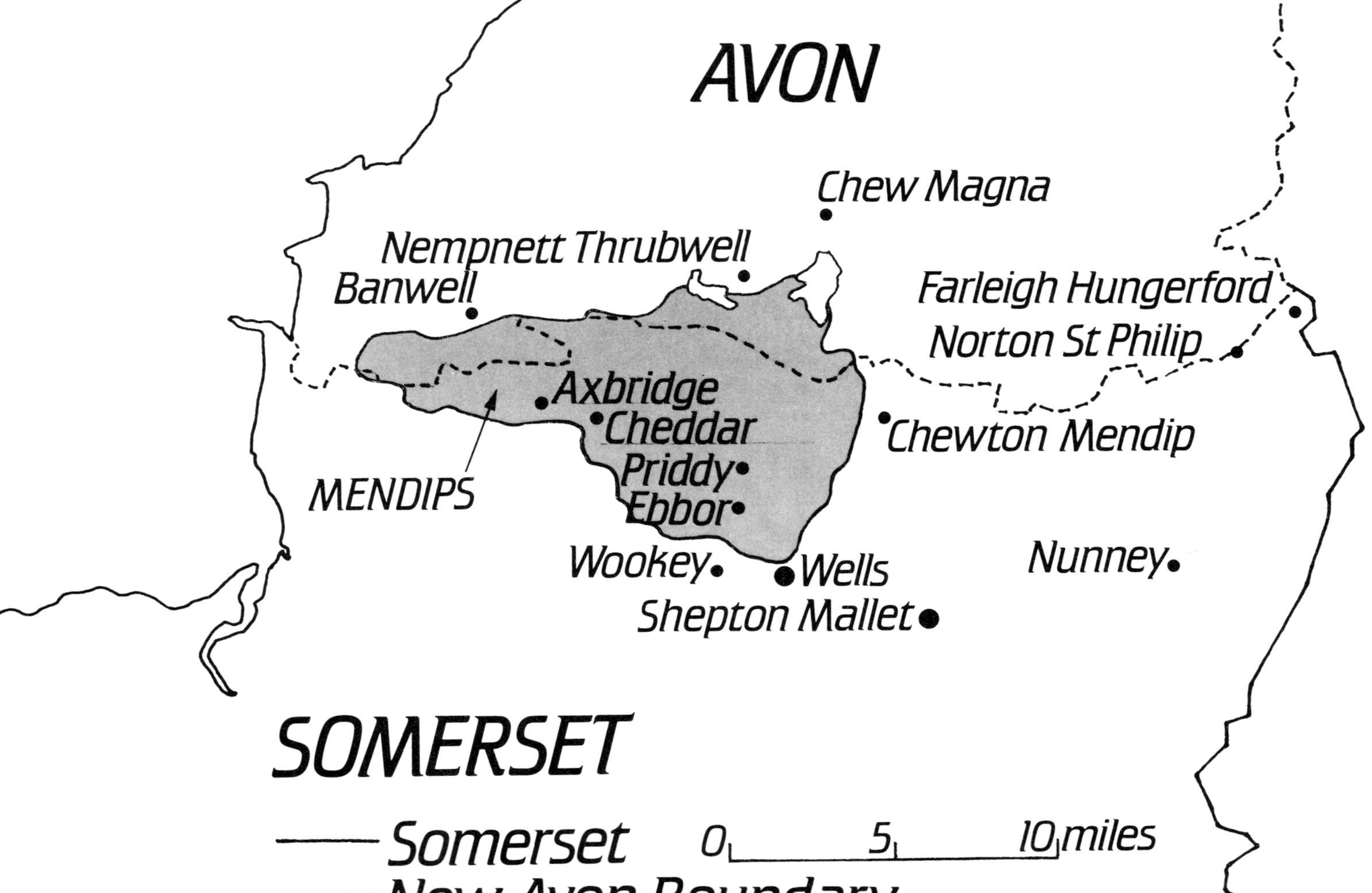
AVON
Chew Magna
Nempnett Thrubwell
Banwell
Farleigh Hungerford
Norton St Philip
Axbridge
Cheddar
Priddy
Ebbor
Chewton Mendip
MENDIPS
Wookey
Wells
Nunney
Shepton Mallet
SOMERSET
Somerset
New Avon Boundary
0
5
10 miles

The Mendips and the North

The Mendips are the limestone hills that run for twenty miles of almost continuous elevation across the county, rising dramatically from flat plains to belie their height of just over a thousand feet at the highest point at Black Down. Affording wonderful views, it is a wild and bleak plateau with a feeling of prehistory in the hill forts of the Beaker Folk and Stone Age people who lived there centuries ago, and in some part remain. The Priddy Nine Barrows and Priddy Stone Circles, each about two hundred yards across are set in a straight line almost a mile long. Legend claims that Christ spent part of His 'lost years' here and many experience a deep sense of religious feeling.

On a 'modern' note, a Sheep Fair has been held here since 1348 when, because of plague, it was transferred from Wells. Hurdles, with a thatched roof to protect them, are always kept on Priddy Green, ready for the summer fair each August. And Priddy has its own gastronomic delicacy — Priddy snails — ordinary garden snails known locally as Wallfish!

To the west is Banwell Hill with a prehistoric earthwork, Banwell Camp, once inhabited by the Goidel-Celts several hundred years before Christ. Within this is a great turf cross, raised to about two feet above the ground with four arms each four feet wide pointing to the four quarters of the compass. It is not known who built it or why, but legend claims the devil kept raising gales which blew down every upright cross the villagers erected so to foil him they laid a cross on the ground. A duller theory is that the cross was connected with a Roman survey, and some think it was a medieval rabbit warren!

Left: Map of the Mendips and Northern Somerset.

Banwell village is of great antiquity and the cave of William Beard, found there in 1824, revealed much prehistoric treasure including the bones of a cave lion. The cave is now closed but the treasures are in Taunton Museum.

Two miles from Cheddar is Black Rock — quiet, sheltered and unspoilt. Once it was part of a medieval forest, a royal hunting trail and an historic trail going back two thousand years when it was a track leading to the Roman silver and lead mines at Charterhouse.

Crook Peak, or pointed hilltop, stands some 628 feet above sea level with a jagged limestone head etched by time and weather. It affords wonderful views and is well worth the effort to climb to its summit. Others believe the Iron Age fort at Maesbury Castle offers the most exciting views of the Somerset countryside. It crowns a hill and is impressive; the outline of the original fortifications of this once impregnable fortress can be clearly seen.

The Mendips are beautiful, mysterious and exhilarating, even inspiring. The Gorge at Burrington Combe was the inspiration for the Reverend Toplady to compose the well-known hymn, *Rock of Ages*, while sheltering from a storm.

Axbridge, near Cheddar is an unspoilt market town full of charm and interest, nestling against the limestone cliff rising behind it. Once the resting place for royal hunting parties after a chase on the Mendip plateau, it gained royal favour and borough status by the reign of Edward the Confessor.

The High Street is twisting, leading to the square, with medieval buildings on either side, the most famous being King John's Hunting Lodge, now the property of the National Trust and open as a museum. King John owned the Royal Forest of Mendip and Cheddar and the timber-framed house was attributed to him though it was built, as a merchant's house, three hundred years after his death. Another of the county's wool towns, its speciality was knitted stockings.

The museum has many local archaeological and geological items from nearby caves on show including the skeleton of a man from a post-Roman cemetery believed to have suffered from spina bifida. The Regency Town Hall has many of the town's treasures and oddities from the past ranging from stocks, bull-baiting anchor to which the animal was tied for this cruel sport, ale taster's glass, branding irons for cattle marked 'AX' for Axbridge to a money changers' table dated 1627. There is an impressive church with a

Trees in a winter landscape.

nave ceiling of exceptional beauty and the old Somerset town seems to personify traditional England, and is a natural for television at Christmas time in the market square.

Cheddar is one of the most remarkable scenes in Britain. The best way to approach is from Priddy when the ravine of limestone walls which rise almost vertically, with a narrow twisting road, ends in the gorge which cuts a cleavage in the edge of the Mendips and ends in the village. If one descends into the ravine from the top, the cliffs seem to increase in grandeur, the best being the last. Like some fantastic castle rising over four hundred feet, with, near the entrance of the 'pass' a mass of rock resembling a crouching lion mounting everlasting guard. Another rock formation looks like a monkey. At the foot of Lion Rock a sheet of water is fed by underground streams, and there is a series of world-famous caves at the entrance to the valley. These date from the Stone Age world of ten thousand years ago, and the stalagmite and stalactite formations are of great beauty and rich in colour. The bones of a prehistoric man were found in 1903 and also bones of long-extinct animals.

People are so fascinated by the gorge and the caves that the village is often overlooked except by the tourists. There was once a Saxon royal palace here which has been reconstructed and can be seen in the Caves Museum. The centre of the village is marked by a fifteenth-century medieval preaching cross, surrounded by a sixteenth-century colonnade of six arches. It is set in the former market place from which several roads radiate, and at one time travellers, merchants and others paid rent for the use of the cross. Cheddar was a busy wool centre.

The Church of St Andrew dates back to the fifteenth century with a tower rising to a hundred feet. It occupies an historic site, the remains of a Roman villa being excavated in the grounds of the vicarage.

Hannah More's old whitewashed cottage is open to view. She did much for her country and for Cheddar in the founding of its first day school in 1789.

Cheese making flourished in the sixteenth century, though it is recorded in the Domesday Book that the royal manor possessed only one cow. Many early cheeses were made of sheep's milk. Daniel Defoe, passing through, said Cheddar cheese was the best in England and many would agree with him today. It is widely imitated — unsuccessfully!

Another culinary delight is the dark red Cheddar strawberries which have been grown here since the last century.

Reservoirs attract many birds and the deepness of the water at Cheddar brings aquatic birds which are a delight to ornithologists.

There is a charming flower — the Cheddar Pink — which only

Cheddar Gorge: 'If one descends into the ravine from the top, the cliffs seem to increase in grandeur . . .'

grows wild in the gorge and was a favourite with Victorian tourists who loved its sweet smell. It is a rarity today.

The Castle of Comfort Inn is isolated, being at the meeting of the roads from Priddy, Harptree and Chewton Mendip. It was originally patronised by workers in the now disused lead mines and was one of four such inns. The inn was said to have been built around a tree, which can be seen in the bar, but more likely, a tree trunk was used as a ceiling support.

Right: 'Chewton Mendip . . . dominated by the 126-foot-high tower of the Church of St Mary Magdalene which was built by Carthusian monks and is one of the finest in Somerset.' Below: Trees seen against a Somerset sky in November.

Chewton Mendip is a former lead mining village with a history dating back to the time of Alfred. It is dominated by the 126-foot-high tower of the Church of St Mary Magdalene which was built by Carthusian monks and is one of the finest in Somerset. It was started in 1441 and took over two years to complete. The church was originally Saxon, and once a Benedictine monastery was near. A rare possession, near the altar, is a stone seat, known as a 'frid', for those, especially criminals, who took sanctuary. It is one of three such seats still said to remain in England. The door has a closing ring, another unusual feature.

Ebbor Gorge was formed millions of years ago when pressure from the earth's crust pushed a strip of grit beneath the limestone to form an impermeable floor over which a river once flowed. It made a wooded chasm, now part of a huge nature reserve and claimed to be the loveliest and most unspoilt gorge in the whole Mendips.

In May 1967 Ebbor Gorge was given to the nation by Mrs G. W. Hodgkinson as a memorial to Sir Winston Churchill and there is a simple stone to the great man in the reserve. A sort of 'miniature Cheddar', it offers caves which housed New Stone Age peoples about 3000 BC, and remains of bears, reindeer and other animals were found. Today there is a profusion of flowers and trees and there are badger setts in the woods. This national nature reserve is a wild and lonely place, tree-shaded and with one steep part called Deer Leap — it is surely one the artist in Sir Winston would have liked to paint.

For millions of years the River Axe wore away the limestone to form the caves known as Wookey Hole. They were inhabited by Stone Age hunters who left evidence of their occupancy, and the chambers contain many colourful stalagmites and stalactites. One of these stalagmites is called the Witch of Wookey, a woman who lived in the caves with her familiars, a goat and a kid. Legends claim she had been crossed in love and vindictively cast spells over the villagers of Wookey. The frightened people appealed to the Abbot of Glastonbury for help and a monk was sent to the caves. The witch, on seeing him, turned to run away, but the monk

Right: 'Ebbor Gorge was given to the nation by Mrs G.W. Hodgkinson as a memorial to Sir Winston Churchill and there is a simple stone to the great man . . .'

quickly sprinkled her with holy water and she was turned to stone and stands there to this day, a brooding frightening figure. Excavations in 1912 revealed the bones of a Romano-British woman, also a goat and kid, and there are witch relics now on show in Wells museum.

Another legend claims a giant conger eel — thirty feet long — hides in the waters of Wookey Hole. The creature swam up the Severn to become King, but he destroyed so many fish he was driven into Wookey Hole by angry fishermen and never escaped. So Wookey has its own 'Loch Ness' monster lurking in the dark waters!

The Hyena Cave was once the haunt of mammoths, lions and

Right: Clevedon when the visitors have gone.
Below: Witch's Dog at Wookey Hole. Legend claims that the witch cast spells over the villagers.

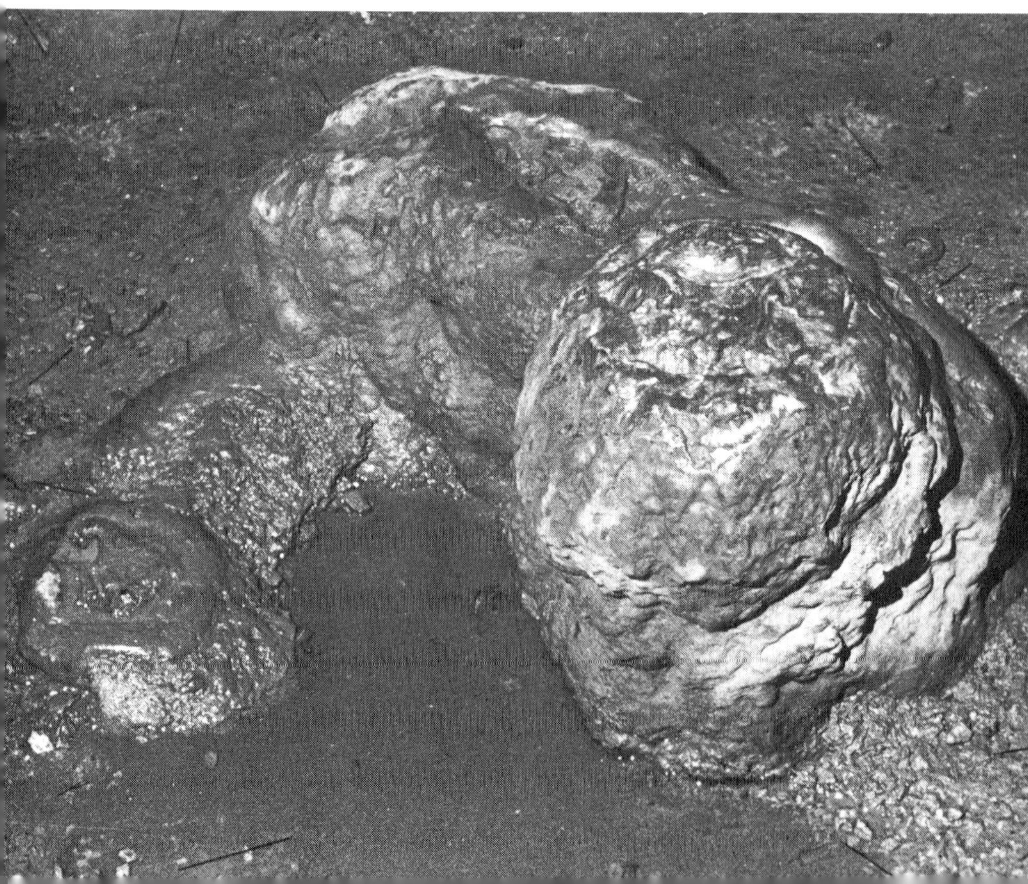

bears at the time of the Stone Age people and the name Wookey means animal trap.

There are other interests at Wookey in the paper-making mill, Madame Tussaud's Waxworks Store and a Fairground Collection that originally belonged to Lady Bangor.

Wells is England's smallest city, the status being granted by Queen Elizabeth II in 1974, and it has one of the most beautiful cathedrals in the country. The three towers stand out against the background of the Mendips and the west front is magnificent. Twice as wide as it is high, it still has nearly three hundred medieval groups of sculpture across the whole façade. Many were destroyed by the Puritans and by the passing of time, but much restoration has taken place. In 1978 the cathedral celebrated its eight hundredth anniversary.

Left: Some of the medieval faces on the front of Wells Cathedral.
Below: The Bishop's Palace, Wells.

Above: The majestic moat at Wells.
Right: A Bishop's swan at Wells.

There are many features. The astronomical clock was made in 1390 and is one of the oldest working clocks in the world. Its dial is over six feet across and moving models of mounted knights joust every quarter of an hour knocking one another off their horses. The figure of Jack Blandifer has sat high above the knights for over five hundred years, kicking his heels to make them move. The clock was possibly made at Glastonbury Abbey by a monk called Peter Lightfoot.

The memorials are many and varied, and the chapel of St Martin is a memorial to every Somerset man who fell in World War I. The nave is breathtaking with many things to see in the south transept — carvings of thieves stealing apples and being caught, for instance. The east window, called the Golden Window, is dated

1339. There are cloisters, a chapter house and a library dated 1425. It is 168 feet in length and possibly the largest medieval one in England, containing archives from the tenth century and chained books on its shelves.

The Bishop's Palace in the centre of the city dates from 1206 and has a battlemented wall and wide moat with a fourteenth-century gatehouse. There is a drawbridge and the swans who live in the moat ring a bell with their beaks when they want feeding which makes a wonderful tourist attraction. The Glastonbury Chair is on view and there is a chapel of great beauty, but the Bishop lives elsewhere.

The College of Vicars, known as the Vicars' Close, was founded in 1348 and is the oldest inhabited street in Western Europe. An unique feature is the bridge over the road leading out of the hall, enabling the vicars to go direct to the church.

Wells market place has two gateways, one called Penniless Porch because in former days so many beggars frequented it, stopping the passers-by for alms. The second leads to the Bishop's Palace.

There are old inns and a modern note in the market place commemorates the feat of a local girl, Mary Rand's Olympic Gold Medal at the Tokyo Olympic Games in 1964. Her winning long jump of 22 feet 2½ inches is marked on the pavement, and twenty years ago was Britain's first Olympic Gold Medal in the long jump and a world record. A pair of gates at the city's athletics ground also mark her feat. Mary, who was educated at Millfield School, now lives with her former Olympic decathlon champion husband Bill and two daughters in California. However, in December 1984 Mrs Toomey, as she now is, came back to Wells to become the first President of the Wells Harriers, and, of course, she was photographed standing on 'her' pavement, wearing her medal, in her home town, watched by her mother who now lives at Street.

St Cuthbert's Church is of Saxon foundation and a magnificent example of the Perpendicular period. The life of the city centred

Left: Wells is steeped in history.
Below: Old tombstone outside Christon Church, a true Somerset curiosity.

Two angles of a street which is reputed to be the oldest occupied street in all Europe.

round the church, and prisoners from the Monmouth Rebellion were kept there for a while. The City Inn was once a gaol. The Wells Museum is near to the cathedral and contains many exhibitions of interest including the Early Iron Age Collection from Wookey Hole.

Shepton Mallet was once a thriving wool centre and its name is derived from Sheeptun, the enclosure into which sheep were driven for safety. The Royal Bath and West Show held here annually maintains the agricultural links.

The Tudor market cross dominates the market place with a labyrinth of little streets leading to it, and the Shambles, or open market stalls are a feature. There is a small museum of local history in the High Street.

The Church of St Peter and St Paul is late fifteenth-century and has one of the finest timber roofs in all England. The three hundred and fifty carved panels are all of different design, and there are thirty-six carved angels along the sides. The pulpit is cut from a single stone and reached by steps. There is an unusual brass of 1649 of Joan and William Strode and their nine children with the skeleton of Death in their midst aiming a dart at the wife!

The font is very old and was rescued from a garden where it had been used as a flower pot!

At Nempnett Thrubwell there is a burial mound known as the Fairy Toot. Originally one of the biggest in the county — sixty yards long, twenty yards broad and fifteen high — it had rows of cells with human bones and horses' teeth. Over the centuries it has been gradually dismantled and little remains. Many came in the past as it was said to be a place known for curing warts.

The fifteenth-century George Inn at Norton St Philip was believed to have been the wool store of the priory of Hinton

Charterhouse. The half-timbered medieval building has oriels and bay windows and was much used by merchants coming to the cloth fair in the town in the Middle Ages. The Duke of Monmouth was there during the Rebellion and escaped when a bullet was aimed at him through a window. Other features include a long gallery at the back and an outside staircase. It is believed to be one of the oldest licensed inns in England.

The church is also fifteenth-century with an extraordinary tower seemingly made up of oddments left over from other ecclesiastical buildings. There is an effigy of an unknown lawyer, dated around 1460, in a gown with an elaborate tomb, and the pointed toes of his shoes curl over the back of a dog!

Samuel Pepys stayed at the George and records that he visited the grave of the Siamese twins, known as the Fair Maids of Foscot, whose bodies were joined 'at the belly'.

At Farleigh Hungerford on the border of the county, there are the ruins of a medieval castle at the edge of a deep ravine. It was once vast and impregnable, moated on one side with the ravine on the other. There is a gatehouse, two towers and a fourteenth-century chapel, now a museum with a collection of armour and weapons. There is a chantry behind a grille with tombs and monuments to the Hungerford family. The best is a fifteenth-century tomb with life size effigy of Sir Thomas Hungerford and his wife. A friend of John of Gaunt, he was the first Speaker of the House of Commons and the builder of the castle.

In the chapel near the altar is a fifteenth-century wall painting of St George battling with a dragon and Crusader relics and arms on the walls.

At Nunney there is a ruined medieval castle in an almost fairy-tale setting with a ten-foot-deep moat and stream surrounding it, forming an island which is now a bird sanctuary.

The castle was built in the fourteenth century (1373) by Sir John de la Mere and modelled on the Bastille in France. In the Civil War it was attacked by the Roundheads, the walls breached and forced to surrender. On Christmas Day 1910 the north wall, breached by the Roundheads, collapsed. To see it is to step back in time and cross the moat, locking up on leaving!

Left: Wear of centuries on these ancient steps at Wells.

Mells is said to be the origin of the childhood rhyme about little Jack Horner, and has a lovely church dating from the fifteenth century. Its bells ring every four hours, night and day from the tower, with four tunes and a special Mells tune and a Christmas one. The church tower rises to one hundred and four feet and inside the church is a chapel to the Horner family who have lived at the Manor since the sixteenth century. The centre of the chapel is dominated by an equestrian statue to Edward Horner, who fell at Cambrai in 1917, by Sir Alfred Munnings. There is also a memorial to Raymond Asquith, son of the Prime Minister, who was killed in France in 1916.

Chew Magna, once a small town, is surrounded by streams and some of the old houses have raised pavements. Dating from medieval times the church is unusual with a huge door with two hundred studs, scratch dials, gargoyles and rare monuments which span the centuries. The earliest is the fourteenth-century carved oak effigy to Sir John de Hauteville, said to have been a man of great strength who threw the Hauteville Quoit, an ancient standing stone, from the top of Maes Knoll to its present resting place near Chew Magna. His vivid effigy is one of the few wooden figures in England.

A fifteenth-century memorial remembers a giant — Sir John St Loe — measuring 7 feet 4 inches in length and 2 feet 4 inches across, a colossal figure with a lion under his feet. Beside him lies his little wife with a small dog and both are wearing neck chains. There is a 'fashionable' sixteenth-century Elizabethan tomb of Edward Baber and his wife — he wearing the gown of a lawyer and she a Paris cap.

In the village an Ale House is known as the Old School House, and the Old Bakehouse had a long handled baker's shovel on the wall outside.

Chew Tower is a castellated folly built in 1770 and stands on Dundry Hill with fine views over the countryside on a clear day.

Right: A young birdlover at Wells.

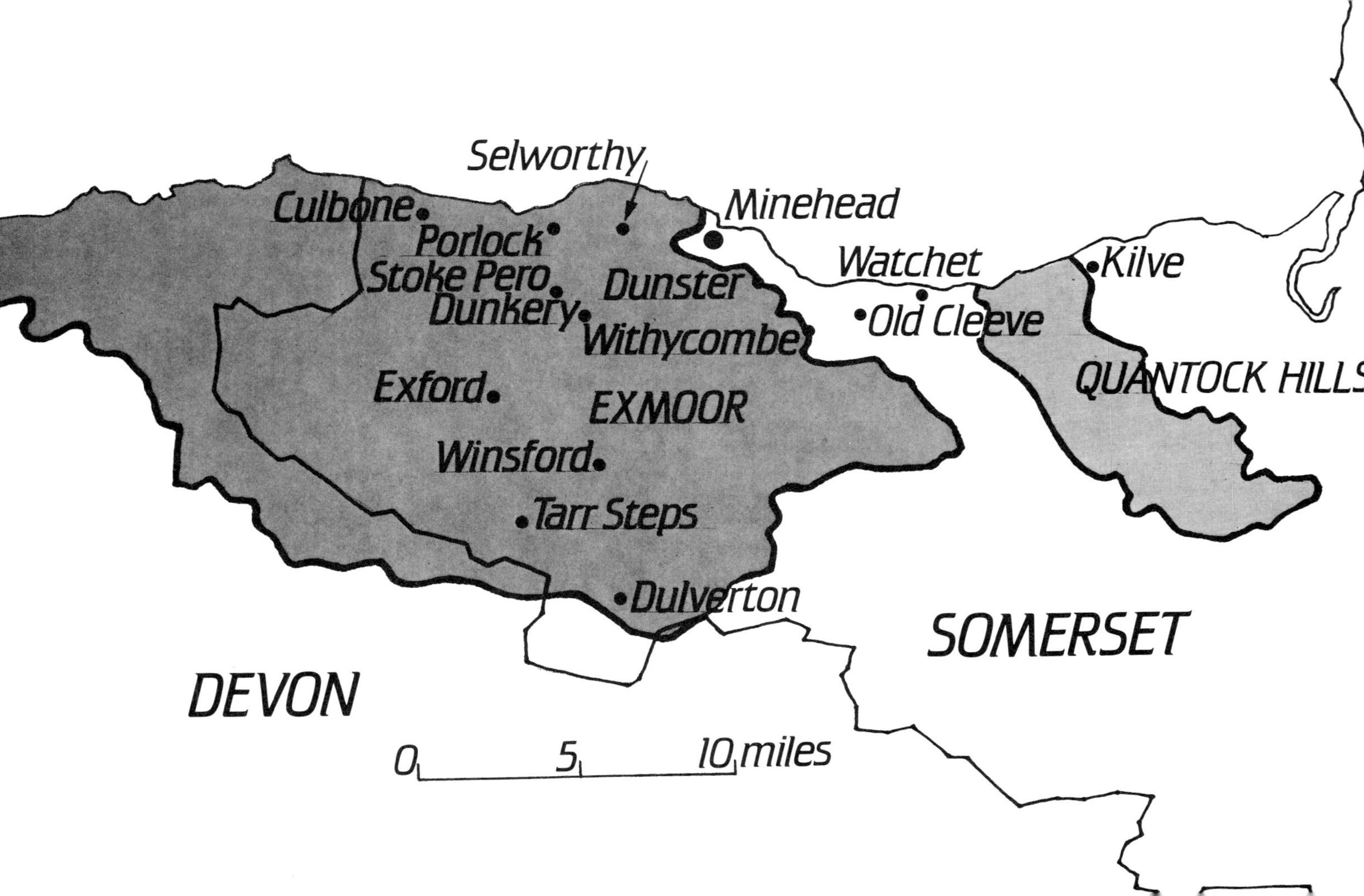
Selworthy
Minehead
Culbone
Porlock
Stoke Pero
Dunster
Dunkery
Withycombe
Watchet
Kilve
Old Cleeve
QUANTOCK HILLS
Exford
EXMOOR
Winsford
Tarr Steps
Dulverton
SOMERSET
DEVON
0
5
10 miles

The Quantocks, the Coast and Exmoor

The Quantocks are rolling, rounded hills west of the Somerset Plain. There are deep wooded valleys, rich in trees — oak, ash, rowan, thorn, and beech — the trees that were once England's pride are all to be found here. The heather-clad moors are an enchantment.

The highest point is Will's Neck, rising to 1,260 feet, on a ridge affording fantastic views. The name means 'ridge of the Welshman', probably referring to a Saxon tribe who fought a battle there.

Somerset's coastal towns are few. Watchet is a small port on the Bristol Channel and in Saxon times was often raided by the Danes. On the Williton road there is a spot called 'Battle Gore' which preserves the memory of a fight with invaders. Watchet was once fortified with its own mint.

Now it is a gentle place with its own charm lying at the foot of Exmoor and the Quantock and Brendon Hills. A coloured alabaster is found on the cliffs of Blue Anchor Bay and gave rise to the name of Watchet Blue. In the past, it was a colour much favoured by gentlemen and King Charles I is said to have had a coat in this shade.

Coleridge, on a visit to the Wordsworths, was said to have been so inspired by the harbour he made it the point of embarkation of the 'Ancient Mariner' is his famous poem.

St Decuman, to whom the fifteenth-century church is dedicated, is said to have floated in from Wales on a raft with his faithful cow and lived as a hermit. Some say he officiated at the marriage of Arthur and Guinevere. The church stands high on a ridge, and its eighty-foot-high battlemented tower, which overlooks the town,

Left: Map of Exmoor and the Coast.

'Exmoor is for some the essence of Somerset . . .'

made an important landmark. There is much of interest inside — a six-hundred-year-old Cross, a brass 'portrait gallery' of the Wyndham family and a glass dated 1273.

In the Civil War a rare event occurred. The Royalists held the port and reinforcements were sent by sea to assist in the siege of Dunster Castle. Unfortunately, the tide was on the ebb and a troop of Roundheads rode into the shallows and forced the ship to surrender, so a ship at sea was taken by a troop of horse.

The old market house, near the harbour, is now a local history museum with models of ships. Watchet is an old, old place with a long history and charm.

If you leave Watchet go towards Washford and do not overlook Old Cleeve where there is a lovely five-hundred-year-old church. An unusual monument dating from the fifteenth century shows an unknown man in a loose gown, a cat crouching at his feet with its paw on a struggling rat. And in the churchyard is a blacksmith's epitaph to George Jones:

My fire's extinct, my forge decayed
And in the dust my body's laid

Cleeve Abbey was founded in 1198 by William, Earl of Lincoln and was the only Cistercian abbey in Somerset. Henry II granted it 'wreck rights' where parts of the estate were damaged by sea, and there were often disputes over spoils from wrecked ships.

There is an inscription over the gatehouse welcoming any visitors — *Gate Stand Open, nor be shut to any honest man* — and though the monastery was dissolved in 1537 the surviving buildings are of interest. The refectory is particularly fine and frescoes can be seen of saints in the buttery nearby. The floor tiles are intricately decorated, and the whole complex provides a fascinating glimpse of life in far off days, and it is one of the few to survive almost intact.

The refectory, with light from high windows, is beautiful with its original roof and stairs for the reader's pulpit, and offers a sense of tranquillity. A church once stood on the north side but only the foundations are traceable.

Kilve, near Watchet, with hills behind and the sea in front, has a long history. Once famous for its smuggling, the chantry chapel was said to have been burned down because of the contraband stored in it.

The villagers armed with stakes and with dogs hunted huge conger eels on the shore each autumn — a sport known as 'glatting'. And on the shore a St Keyna Serpent may be seen — not as legend claims a snake turned to stone — but an ammonite.

Wordsworth found the place an inspiration and wrote of 'Kilve by the green sea' and Southey of the shore in their poetry immortalising this rocky place.

For twenty-eight years (from 1910–1938) the parish had a sporting Rector in the person of the Reverend D. Hartwell James who was nationally renowned as a wet fly trout fisherman. A sporting man with a keen eye and a good shot, he disliked hunting, and unlike many of his fellow clergymen at the time did not join in the local sport. It is said he subtly rebuked those who followed the chase by choosing hymns such as *As pants the hart* at the start of the hunting season as a reminder of his dislike.

Minehead is the largest of Somerset's coastal resorts and it is also the most westerly town in the county and one of the oldest. Its name 'mynedd' means a hill, and it is situated round a wide curving bay in the mouth of the Bristol Channel, making it a safe harbour. The old part of the town, Quay Town, rises up the slopes of North Hill and the pier of 1616 was incorporated into the harbour. It was a busy port trading with Wales for cattle, sheep, wool, butter, fish and coal and the town's arms show a woolpack and a sailing ship. Herrings were once a major export, but after the fish left the waters the trade ceased. Smuggling was rife at Burgundy Combe nearby and there are ruins of an old chapel and hermitage.

A cellar with long beams, near the Quay, is the Chapel of St Peter, dating from 1628 where prayers are offered for those at sea.

Left: Some distinctive Dunster architecture — 'one of the most photographed places in Somerset.'

This was once a storeroom, but its owner, Robert Quirke, dedicated a ship and its cargo to God's service after being in a violent storm at sea. He was one of the town's benefactors and provided almshouses protected by a curse against conversion to other use than by the poor.

St Michael's Church on the North Hill was built some five hundred years ago and had a beacon light in the tower for ships approaching the harbour.

At the foot of the steps to the hill are old cottages and one house, with iron bars on the windows, was used as a prison in Elizabethan times and later as a workhouse.

A rarity in the shopping centre is a statue of the last Stuart sovereign, Queen Anne, and worth noticing. It was given to the town by a Swede who was Member of Parliament in nine parliaments.

Minehead continues a Somerset tradition — originally meant to have driven off the Danes in the past — with its Hobby Horse — Obby Oss — on May Day each year. For three days, sometimes with three horses — Dunster Horse, Sailors' Horse and Town Horse — followed by attendants, drums and accordions, this gaily coloured 'thing' rushes at bystanders in a mischievous way to perform ancient fertility rites and collect money. It is supposed to bring bad luck to refuse payment!

To visit Porlock is an adventure. A hairpin bend with a one-in-four gradient, one of the steepest hills in Britain, has been the death knoll of many a car, but when the journey is over, the village is attractive. There are small, whitewashed cottages with tall chimneys and a gentle air.

Porlock's church is thirteenth-century and dedicated to St. Dubricus, and is said to have a fragment of a Saxon cross in the nave. The fourteenth-century effigy of a knight, John Harrington, lies beside his wife. He fought alongside Henry V in France in 1417.

The area is popular for walking and horse riding. Life is leisurely here and a notice on a stable door has a request for quietness and a reminder that horses are resting inside.

The inhabitants of Porlock beat off invading Danes in 918 and the Saxons raided in 1058. Today boats can no longer reach Porlock itself, now well inland, but at Porlock Weir is one of Somerset's most attractive harbours, retaining an air of simplicity.

Low tide at Porlock Weir, showing the channel in to the old lock.

The beach at Porlock Weir.

The Ship Inn at Porlock was once the haunt of wreckers and smugglers, and the Poet Laureate, Robert Southey, wrote of its comforts in a verse 'written by the alehouse fire' while staying there on one of his many visits to the Westcountry.

In 1899, during a storm on 12 January, the Lynmouth lifeboat was launched from the Weir to rescue some shipwrecked sailors. The storm was so fierce the boat could not put out from Lynmouth and had to be hauled by men and horses, negotiating both Countisbury and the infamous Porlock Hill, to the Weir where the water in the bay was less rough.

A small fifteenth-century manor house called Doverhay is in the main street of Porlock and, though once a family home, is now used as an information centre, even possessing a billiards room.

On a ledge above the bank of Colley Water near Porlock is an impressive stone circle about eighty feet in diameter consisting of ten standing stones and eleven flat stones. Although some of the stones are missing, they are clearly in a ring, and near a small barrow, resembling a miniature Stonehenge. The date is uncertain.

The reason and use of the stone circles has not been fully discovered though they are almost peculiar to Britain and vary in design and age. The circle near Porlock belongs to the same tradition as the circle at Withypool and both stand near ridgeways but have not been excavated.

Exmoor is, for some, the essence of Somerset, and its beauty as a moorland is unrivalled. The large area of over three hundred square miles — one third is in Devonshire — is a landscape with everything — secret valleys, woods, rivers, deer, wild ponies, birds and excitement. Called by some the 'Alps of Somerset', it is a place of contrast with farmland, wild parts crowned with crunchy purple heather like coloured sheets, secret streams, wonderful loneliness and timelessness. It has a darker side. The numerous burial grounds of prehistoric peoples who lived there, the treacherous boggy plateau called 'The Chains' — the whole is steeped in legend.

An Exmoor bridge near Luccombe.

Oare Church, a dramatic setting in R.D. Blackmore's novel Lorna Doone.

The belief in witchcraft has been strong over the centuries and the necessity to placate the fairies. They must never be crossed, and it was an old custom to leave bread and milk for them as a reward for favours. The fairies were believed to have stopped Moolham Church being built, so it was never wise to rouse their anger.

Exmoor is a region of contrast — a place to explore again and again for one never tires of its beauty, strength and the sense of eeriness that creeps over it. Red deer and wild ponies roam its vastness.

Many prehistoric barrows, some named, some numbered, can be seen and one called Setta has a boundary wall through it. There are mounds and stone circles at Brendon Common, and one circle was

Left: The bridge at Malmsmead: the heart of Lorna Doone country. Below: Exmoor mare and foal.

found recently by chance in woodland at Culbone Row. This consists of twenty stones, about knee high, suggesting a prehistoric single row. The Culbone Stone, discovered lying flat in 1940 and re-erected is a little distance from the Row and is inscribed with a wheeled cross on its face, askew on the stone, and dating from the Dark Ages.

There are isolated churches such as Stoke Pero and Culbone and scatterings of farmsteads. Stoke Pero is the earliest known Christian settlement on the moor. A jingle once ran:

Culbone, Oare and Stoke Pero
Parishes three no parson'll go.

One parson in the fourteenth century is said to have carried off the wife of a parishioner!

Above: A Dulverton event captured by a photographer years ago.
Right: Bury village, near Dulverton.

Culbone is one of the smallest parish churches in England. It is thirty-five feet long, twelve feet wide with stout Norman walls, a waggon roof, shingled spire, two bells — one fourteenth century — and oak screen. The sound of the sea below can be heard, as it is set in an almost secret place between the sea and hilltops rising to thirteen hundred feet. It is difficult to find and has to be approached on foot, up an old pack horse path. But the climb and effort are worth it. Its loneliness is shared by many including Coleridge who is said to have 'dreamed' *Kubla Khan* there and then written it.

There are few houses in the centre of Exmoor which is characterised by rough moorland and some cultivated land. Those exploring on horseback or foot experience its real loneliness.

It is true the Doones were an invention of R. D. Blackmore in

Lorna Doone, but long before his novel was written, stories abounded of robbers, said to be Cavaliers fleeing Cromwell, Scots or just robbers. The area is perfect for such a tale. For many, *Lorna Doone* is a reality.

Exmoor ponies, descendants of the native British wild horses, are believed to have roamed the moor from earliest times to the present day. They possess strength, courage and endurance and there is an annual round-up and sale in the autumn.

The villages are scattered and of those worth visiting the Horner Valley offers woods, scenery, a packhorse bridge and peace.

Dulverton, the site of Iron Age forts, is also that of trout streams and beautiful scenery. Dunkery is the highest point on the moor rising to over 1,700 feet above sea level. Its beacon was lit in 1558 to warn of the Spanish Armada and has also been lit at times of national rejoicing. In the nineteenth century it was the custom to climb the beacon to watch the Easter Morning sunrise from the top. From here one can see for miles. And it is a custom to add a stone to the cairn on the top, just for luck.

Withycombe is a cobbled village with an aisleless thirteenth-century church. Under a window a stone figure of a widow is seven hundred years old, with richly carved vases at her head and feet. But hidden in a wall recess there is a man from the Middle Ages. He

Above: The eight-sided Yarn Market at Dunster in August 1984.
Left: The same scene in more leisurely days.

is unknown with long hair and wearing a hat which is said to be one of the first hats to appear on a church monument. He is carrying a heartcase to show he died somewhere else and only his heart was brought there for burial.

There is a memorial to Joan Carne who died in 1612, locally credited with being a witch, who murdered three husbands, but her spirit had to be laid!

Dunster is a charming market town steeped in antiquity and one of the most photographed places in Somerset. A castle has been here since Saxon times, given to the Mohun family after the

Above: The lovely facade of the Luttrell Arms at Dunster. Left: Lamp at the Luttrell Arms.

Conquest and sold to the Luttrells in 1376 and given to the National Trust six hundred years later. There are gateways of the fourteenth century and one bearing a Civil War bullet. It was a Royalist stronghold and changed hands more than once as the war continued. At one time it was said to have been the only place in Somerset in the last year of the Civil War flying the royal standard. The skeleton of a giant of some six feet six inches was found manacled to the gatehouse.

The priory church of St George, the largest Exmoor parish, has an unique rood screen, supporting a gallery, the longest in England. The clock chimes every four hours with a different tune each day. There is much evidence of the Luttrell family. The stone

Above: 'Exford is the largest of the highland villages.' Right: Selworthy Church: '. . . windows worthy of a cathedral.'

altar of the monks from the priory remains and there are many other relics of note, including a sloping-topped desk with a brass lock, used by a monk.

Behind is a dovecote from the former priory with its revolving ladder and five hundred nest holes.

The eight-sided Yarn Market has stood since 1600, and nearby a medieval house, once the residence of the Abbot of Cleeve, is now the Luttrell Arms, an attractive pub. It was the headquarters of Blake when he besieged the Castle in the Civil War.

Conygar Hill is topped by a folly 'look-out' tower built in 1776 which makes a striking landmark.

Elworthy has another folly on Willett Hill, a tiny church and a long ridge of Iron Age forts and barrows.

In nearby Sparborough Field a small circle of three-foot-high upright stones was uncovered, with bones in an urn dating from the Bronze Age.

Exford is the largest of the highland villages and well known as the centre of stag hunting with the kennels for hounds there. There is an ancient cross in the churchyard, a memorial to a good Samaritan and another to a sheep stealer. The remains of a prescott or priest's cottage are visible.

Selworthy is known for its thatched cottages and oak trees. The church which lies in a hollow, is fourteenth-century with much to see — 'Windows worthy of a cathedral', graceful arcades and a superb waggon roof, one of the finest in England with the face of Christ looking down among the symbols of His Passion. There is a four-hundred-year-old cross in the churchyard. Selworthy Beacon rises 1014 feet above the sea and is another worth visiting.

Winsford is one of the prettiest villages in the county and set in a wooded valley with a thatched inn and church with a ninety foot

tower. It is on the Exe and the Winn and has six bridges, some of them merely footbridges, more than any other of the villages that challenge it for beauty. The thatched Royal Oak inn makes a perfect setting for the meets of the hunts, and there is one cottage built on rock.

Winsford Hill with Spire Cross and the Wambarrows is said to be a haunted place. And on the hill is a longstone, known as the Caratacus Stone, said to commemorate a chieftain. It was thrown down by vandals in 1923 and re-erected at the wish of Sir Thomas Acland. In the Middle Ages, as the Langeston, it had been a Forest boundary, and there is a Dark Age inscription on the uphill side, maybe indicating that an ancient track ran near, and it may have been a mark of stream worship in the Bronze Age.

The dappling River Barle flows into the River Exe at Dulverton but a few miles away it flows under Tarr Steps, claimed to be the oldest bridge in England and believed to be over two thousand years old. The actual date of its construction has not been determined, but it is an ancient packhorse bridge, 180 feet long

Left: The haunting quality of Somerset.
Below: 'Winsford is one of the prettiest villages in the county.'

with seventeen spans. Legend claims the devil built it, and one tale goes that a cat, running across it, disappeared in a puff of sulphur!

It has a fascination that makes thousands of visitors cross it each year, in spite of its unevenness, maybe thinking of the laden, plodding packhorses who clattered over it in past centuries. In 1952, at the time of the Lynmouth Flood Disaster, a flood swept away some of the stones, but each one has been restored to its original place.

Pinkworthy Pond nearby was made by landowner John Knight and is said to be 'eerie and haunted' after a jilted farm labourer drowned himself in it.

Right: A Dunster gateway in almost Mediterranean sunlight. Below: Ancient Tarr Steps — a real Westcountry curiosity.

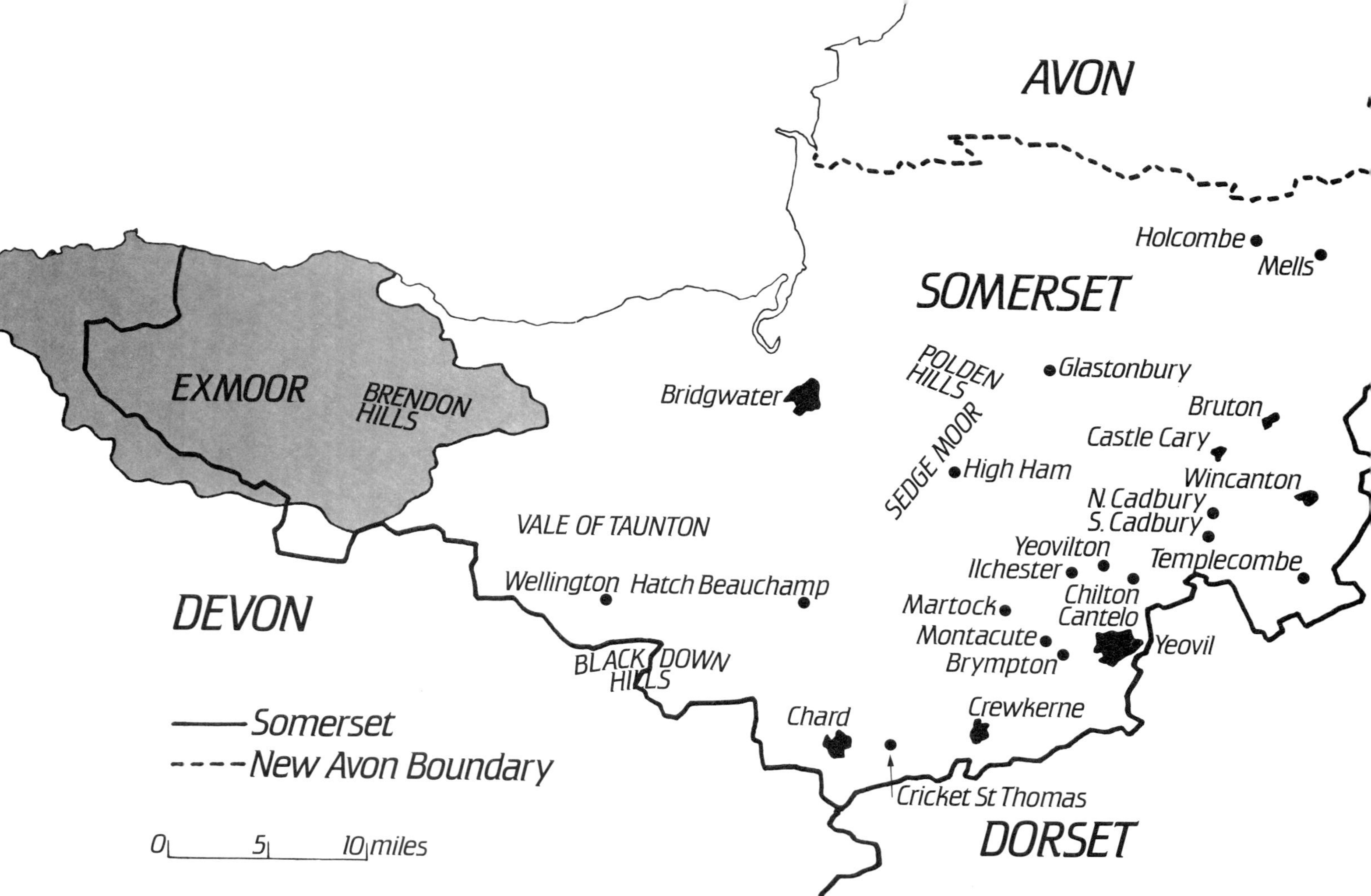
AVON
SOMERSET
Holcombe
Mells
Glastonbury
POLDEN HILLS
Bridgwater
Bruton
Castle Cary
SEDGE MOOR
High Ham
Wincanton
N. Cadbury
S. Cadbury
EXMOOR
BRENDON HILLS
VALE OF TAUNTON
Yeovilton
Ilchester
Templecombe
Wellington
Hatch Beauchamp
Chilton Cantelo
Martock
DEVON
Montacute
Yeovil
Brympton
BLACK DOWN HILLS
Chard
Crewkerne
Somerset
New Avon Boundary
Cricket St Thomas
DORSET
0
5
10 miles

Hills, Levels and the South

There are three other hill ranges in Somerset — the Brendon, the Blackdown and the Poldens, but they have been overshadowed by the beauty of the Quantocks and the excitement of the Mendips with its gorges and caves.

The Brendons, nearer to Exmoor with red sandstone, were the site of lead mining in Roman times, an industry which continued until the nineteenth century.

The Blackdown are lower with greensand and the water flowing from them was used in industry such as shirt making.

The Poldens are limestone, never rising above three hundred feet.

All three ranges seem to offer protection to the villages and towns and though they lack the grandeur of the Mendips and Quantocks, all have their role to play in Somerset's landscape and history.

Nudging the Blackdown Hills is Wellington. The Iron Duke, victor of the Battle of Waterloo, took his title from this little town, and he is commemorated by a huge obelisk, 175 feet in height, on the Blackdown Hills. It is in the shape of a bayonet, the type used by his armies. A spiral staircase leads to the top and from here one can see the Quantocks, Brendon and Exmoor.

Once a famous cloth-making town, the fifteenth-century church has an elaborate monument to Lord Justice Popham, Speaker of the House of Commons and Lord Chief Justice. He presided at the trials of Guy Fawkes and Sir Walter Raleigh. In a recess the stone figure of a priest was buried six hundred years ago with one of the earliest inscriptions ever written in English on his tomb.

Left: Map of the Somerset Hills, Levels and the South.

Above: 'Nowadays the Norman Castle at Taunton is the Taunton County Museum with much of interest. It is said to be haunted by Monmouth's men, who were imprisoned there . . .'
Right: A shop front decoration in Taunton spotted by photographer Julia Davey.

Nowadays there is a sports centre and ski slope mingling with the Georgian houses.

Taunton is the county town of Somerset and a busy market town, taking its name from the River Tone which flows through the centre.

There is evidence that there has been a market here for over a thousand years, originally in front of the Castle, parts of which are dated from 1300. Nowadays the Norman Castle is the Taunton

County Museum with much of interest. It is said to be haunted by Monmouth's men, who were imprisoned there, and their gaolers.

The Great Hall, where Judge Jeffreys condemned to death five hundred supporters of the Duke of Monmouth is 120 feet in length. The Regimental Museum of the County Regiment is now housed here with outstanding relics of their proud history during many campaigns. Other exhibits include historical and archaeological objects, outstanding Chinese pottery, finds from the Roman Low Ham pavement, the Shapwick boat and other treasures. Witches' relics are also on show together with a gruesome reminder of the Rebellion in a piece of skin.

There is a modern Telecommunications Museum, the earliest exhibit dating from 1877.

St Mary's is the major church with its 163-feet-high tower of red Quantock stone a landmark. The bells play tunes. Joseph Savell, a giant of some seven feet four inches, and weighing thirty-seven stones, was buried in the churchyard in 1929. He made a living

Below left: Holcombe Church.
Below: A curiosity in Somerset stone at Holcombe.

Above: Holcombe Church in its wooded setting. Right: J.C. White bowling for Somerset. His slow bowling looked curiously innocent — but he took more than 2,000 wickets for the county.

walking as a curiosity and went blind and was given a caravan in which to travel. One of his shoes is in the museum.

The Tudor House, called the oldest house in the town, also has the 'presence' of Judge Jeffreys who dined there during the trials.

The home of Somerset County Cricket Club, the atmosphere at the County Ground in Taunton is strong. The main gates bear the initials JCW in memory of the player J. C. White who was a farmer from Stogumber. He captained both Somerset and England, and probably no other farmer has ever done that. His slow bowling looked innocent enough, yet in his career he took more than two thousand wickets for Somerset, and on one famous occasion he bowled out the entire Worcestershire team for just seventy-six runs. John Cornish White, known as Jack, came from sturdy Somerset stock and he had the stamina to go on bowling hour after hour, only going off the field to change his shirt and down a glass of beer!

The Club has in its possession Harold Gimblett's England touring blazer and mounted balls presented to Les Braund. In 1935, Harold Gimblett, a young man on a Somerset farm, won Sir Walter Lawrence's trophy and one hundred guineas prize for scoring the fastest century in only sixty-three minutes.

It is the intention of the Supporters' Club to open a museum of Somerset cricket in the future.

For centuries cider making has been one of Taunton's industries and in the autumn it is possible to watch the process — a great attraction.

Hatch Beauchamp is a village in picturesque surroundings. There is a medieval church with a memorial window to a VC, Colonel Chard, hero of the Rorke's Drift action. Queen Victoria sent a wreath which was preserved beneath. The Zulu War of 1879 aroused much controversy, but will always be remembered because of the incredible heroism of a few British soldiers defending a post at Rorke's Drift.

Isandhlwana, nearby, had been the scene of a massacre by the Zulus and it was vital to prevent the enemy advancing further on Natal. On the 22/23 January 1879 there was a mass attack on the small post at Rorke's Drift which consisted of a store and a hospital, by four thousand Zulus. The garrison, mostly men of the 24th South Wales Borderers, consisted of eight officers and 131 men, many of whom were sick in hospital. The officer commanding was Lieutenant John Rouse Merriott Chard of the Royal Engineers. The engagement lasted for twelve hours, the Zulus attacking relentlessly. When they tried to fire the thatch on the hospital they were repulsed. The British soldiers displayed outstanding gallantry and their officers inspired leadership. Eleven VCs were awarded, including one for Lieutenant Chard, in this epic of endurance and courage.

Reinforcements arrived to find six hundred enemy dead and fifteen of the defenders. Natal was saved. Lieutenant Chard was born in Pathe on 21 December 1847 and later became a Colonel. He died at Hatch Beauchamp on 1 November 1897 and his name was inscribed on the Colour of the 24th Regiment the South Wales Borderers. One of the VCs awarded was later stolen and replaced on the orders of King Edward VII, and another, that of Private Hook, was awarded on the field where he earned it, claiming to be the only survivor to be so honoured at Rorke's Drift by Lord Wolseley.

Hatch Court, an eighteenth-century Palladian mansion is worth a visit with its pictures, staircase, China room, deer park and unusual Canadian Military Museum.

Bridgwater has been in existence for about a thousand years, a settlement originally being formed on the west bank of the River Parrett where it was less likely to flood and also made a good river crossing.

It developed as a river port and a castle was built by William de Bruere, the town gaining Borough status in 1200. The cloth trade flourished in the fifteenth century, but in the Civil War it was the scene of a major siege and the castle and many other buildings were destroyed.

Robert Blake, Admiral and the town's Member of Parliament,

Left: Harold Gimblett on the attack. As a young man on a Somerset farm he won a prize for the fastest century.

Above: 'Bridgwater has been in existence for about a thousand years.'
Right: 'It developed as a river port . . .'

was born there in 1599 and his skills gained England naval supremacy in the time of Cromwell. He was active in pursuing the Royalist fleet and later the Barbary pirates. His birthplace honours him with an imposing statue, his right-hand outstretched, pointing finger to the fore, at the Guildhall. The house in which he was born is now a museum of his life and exploits. It also contains much Somerset family history and many relics from the Battle of Sedgemoor. One wall has the unusual graffiti of a sixteenth-century sailing ship. The Admiral's compass and sea chest are also on show.

An original King's Proclamation of 1685 after the Battle of

Sedgemoor is a rarity and a sword used at Sedgemoor by a thirteen-year-old girl, Mary Bridge. She took it to kill the owner who had insulted her mother, and she was acquitted at her trial and the sword presented to her.

There was once a canal to Taunton used for transporting goods, but the coming of the railways caused its decline and it is nowadays only for recreational use.

In Castle Street is a folly made in 1851 showing the latest innovations in concrete with a painted statue of Napoleon! St Mary's Church is fourteenth-century with a spire rising to 170 feet in height. Monmouth is said to have surveyed the ground of Sedgemoor from here. Behind the altar is an unusual painting of a beardless Christ.

The four day St Matthew's Fair in September — sheep and hill ponies — has been held annually since 1400. The Guy Fawkes Carnival is another big event. The oldest building in the town is

Above: Lock at Bridgwater photographed in the summer of 1984.
Right: St Mary's Church at Bridgwater at 10.30.

said to be the Old Vicarage Restaurant, believed to have been the medieval vicarage and now basically sixteenth-century.

Ilchester was Somerset's main Roman town and was excavated in the 1970s. On the Fosse Way, it was a place of some importance, once possessing the county's only polling station and only jail, being nicknamed 'Jailchester'. There was a Saxon mint, nunnery and friary — all now gone.

Roger Bacon the scientific philosopher, was born here in the thirteenth century. He was a man of great learning, and much interested in experimental science and optics. The town possesses an unique mace dating from the thirteenth century with three kings and an angel on it, and it is the oldest staff of office in England. The

inscription, translated, reads, 'I am a mark of amity: do not forget me.'

Not far away is the village of Chilton Cantelo, named after the Cantilupe family, and it is known because of a grisly relic!

The skull of Theophilus Brome, a native of Warwickshire who came to Somerset to avoid hostility after the Civil War, refuses to be buried. He died in 1670 and requested that his skull be removed from his body and kept in the house threatening a haunting if his wishes were not carried out. His body is in Chilton Cantelo Church and his skull may be found in a cupboard at his home at Higher Chilton Farm where it keeps silence — as long as it is not disturbed.

Martock's twelfth-century church was acquired by the Treasurer of Wells Cathedral in 1227 and he became Rector and Patron.

The Treasurer's house is of Hamstone dating from the thirteenth century and it later became the vicarage until, in the nineteenth century, it passed into private hands. The earliest part is the solar or great hall but the most impressive is the fourteenth-century hall with collar-braced timber roof and five windows of 1330. It is now owned by the National Trust and retains much of its original medieval work.

Sedgemoor is on the 'Levels' and is a low-lying marshy region stretching from the Mendips to Taunton and Ilminster.

In July 1685 the last battle was fought on English soil, between the rebels who followed the Duke of Monmouth and the troops of King James II at Westonzoyland. The battle lasted an hour and a half, but will never be forgotten.

The parish register for this village reads:

> *300 rebels killed. 500 prisoners. 79 wounded.*
> *26 hanged. 16 King's troops killed. 100 wounded.*

The church at nearby Chedzoy bears the marks where Monmouth's men sharpened their swords before battle. The terrible outcome is well-known and a simple memorial stone stands in the

Left: St Mary's Church, Bridgwater. 'Monmouth is said to have surveyed the ground of Sedgemoor from here . . .' There the last battle was fought on English soil, between the rebels and the troops of King James II.

field where many of the slain are buried, but also dedicated to those who fought and suffered the terrible retribution that followed after Judge Jeffreys 'Bloody Assizes' in which he showed no mercy.

A sad, solemn place the battlefield, it still reminds one of the valour and suffering that happened, even though today the fields are drained and peaceful cattle graze contentedly.

The area has a thriving industry in the growing of willows or osiers for basket making, which has been going on for hundreds of years. It is recorded that Somerset is the only county to grow willows, and the craft was first mentioned in 1225 when a murdered man at Langport was described as a 'basket maker'.

Tom Pocock was a successful highwayman in the area in the eighteenth century. After a robbery he escaped up one of the rhines, and it was not until he revealed his secret and was betrayed that his career ended. The sluice gates were opened and he was drowned and is said to haunt the rhine still.

Sedgemoor, the low level area with wide, wide fields and rhines where willows grow and flowers, can lay claim to have played a strong role in English history. It was here that Alfred fought and defeated the Danes when a lagoon stretched inland and villages rested on islands, but it is the defeat of the Duke of Monmouth's armies that is best remembered.

Some of the old rhines are long gone through land reclamation and cultivation, but though it is long since they echoed to the sounds of battle and the cries of the wounded, running red with blood, the sadness prevails, and no amount of birdsong or time can change it.

Near Sedgemoor is Barrow Mump, some nine and a half acres of lonely hill, once Alfred's lookout and said to be haunted. It is crowned by an unfinished eighteenth-century chapel and this is joined to a ruined medieval one. It was given to the National Trust as a memorial to the Somerset men who gave their lives in the Second World War.

And Burrow Bridge on the River Parrett was the last toll bridge in Somerset, being 'freed' in 1946. The old pumping station is now a museum.

Combe Florey church has an interesting brass of 1526 on the tomb of a knight. Sir John de Merriet is shown in armour with shields on each shoulder for added protection. This was after Crusaders had suffered terrible wounds from the Saracens because

A country characteristic — rolled hay.

they lacked it. He has a wife on either side of him, and the heart of an earlier member of the family, a nun, is buried in the north wall, her body being buried elsewhere.

Curry Rivel has a lovely fifteenth-century church facing a green. Notice the stone figure above the porch playing the bagpipes and round the corner is another playing a violin. In the north chapel are family memorials, and above them a stone showing a priest's head on top of a cross, said to date from 1275, the forerunner of church portrait brasses.

Nearby, overlooking Sedgemoor on a hill summit is a plain Doric column designed by Capability Brown for William Pitt, in memory of William Pynsent. Once it was possible to climb it by means of a spiral staircase, but after a cow struggled to the top, had vertigo, fell and crashed to her death over the parapet, it was closed.

Before the Somerset marshes were drained ships could sail inland as far as Glastonbury. The hill on which High Ham village stands was once an island. It makes a notable landmark with its stone windmill with thatched roof above the flatlands. The last survivor of five that once existed in the area, it dates from 1820 but the sails have now gone. Old houses round the Church of St Andrew complete the scene. One of its most striking features is a row of gargoyles with trumpeter, fiddler and piper and a monkey nursing a baby and a man throwing stones.

Low Ham was a Roman site and an unusual mosaic found in a field here depicted the story of Dido and Aeneas and is now in Somerset County Museum.

Brooded over by the Tor, Glastonbury is a glorious conglomerate of tradition, legends, holiness and mystery that almost overwhelm this tranquil Somerset town. To some it is a place for all seasons, and those who come to seek its tranquillity in a renewal of faith can do so. Others — maybe the curious and the sceptical — will merely see it as a beautiful place, something on a tourist itinerary.

Glastonbury Abbey, 1300 years ago, was a well-established foundation, its abbot one of a long, long line stretching back into the mists of antiquity. St Patrick is said to have become a monk there after landing in Cornwall later returning as abbot and buried there.

Glastonbury seems timeless as if it has always been there. It is said that Joseph of Arimathea came, struck his staff into the ground and the famous Thorn has flourished ever since. The relics he brought included the Chalice, said to have been used at the Last Supper, which made a basis for the Arthurian Legend of the Quest of the Holy Grail. When it is rediscovered it is believed there will be a time of peace and enlightenment.

The underworld of fantasy and fairies lays claim to Glastonbury. Their king, Gwynn, leader of the Wild Hunt, had an invisible kingdom said to be on top of the Tor, the gateway to his kingdom, which made it a shrine to be venerated. The spiralling terraces are man-made encouraging the belief that the hill was once a huge Pagan sanctuary, the sacred place being the spring. Named Chalice

Right: Glastonbury: '. . . a glorious conglomerate of tradition, legends, holiness and mystery . . .'

Above: 'It is said that Joseph of Arimathea came, struck his staff into the ground and the famous Thorn has flourished ever since . . .'
Right: Chalice Well, Glastonbury.

Well it is said to have effected miraculous cures and will never run dry. Joseph of Arimathea was said to have placed the Chalice beneath the spring giving it its name.

The Abbey, once one of the richest in the country, is now mainly a ruin with a few gaunt buildings left to enable one to imagine its size and grandeur. St Mary's Chapel dating from 1186 is a shell, with an underground chapel to St Joseph. Within the ruins is a place marking the 'tombs' of King Arthur and Queen Guinevere. In 1965 a tall plain oak Cross from the Duchy of Cornwall estate was erected in the ruins, a gift from the Queen.

The last Abbot, eighty-year-old Richard Whiting, was executed on the Tor. The Glastonbury Chair in which he sat at his trial — copied as chancel furniture in many churches — may be seen at the Bishop's Palace in Wells.

The Chapel of St Patrick within the walls dates from the sixteenth century and includes some original stained glass.

The Abbot's kitchen, built in the fourteenth century, was the place where food for pilgrims and guests was prepared. Many finds from excavations of the Abbey are exhibited here.

The fourteenth-century barn of the Abbey is now the Somerset Rural Life Museum and includes an exhibition showing the life of a Victorian farm labourer from cradle to grave; local folklife and many curiosities such as two shrivelled animals' hearts found in a chimney said to ward off evil spirits.

Churches of note are St Benignus and St John's with the Glastonbury Thorn, sprigs of which are sent to the Queen and Queen Mother at Christmas, in the churchyard.

The Tribunal, a fifteenth-century building in the High Street is

the old Courthouse. Finds from the Iron Age Lake villages include the Glastonbury Bowl and Saw and centuries old wooden artefacts are among the items to be seen in this museum.

The George and Pilgrim Hotel was rebuilt in the fifteenth century by the Abbot for the accommodation of pilgrims. It is one of the few pre-Reformation inns in existence and the longest serving in England. The panels of the doorway are interesting, bearing the arms of the Abbey and Edward IV, the third having been erased. It may have shown a white rose of York and been removed when the Tudors came to power.

Yeovil is in the centre of the midwest and one of the principal industrial towns. It is a busy, bustling place on the way to somewhere with glove making and aircraft making its main industries. Its parish church is known as the 'lantern of the West' because of the number and size of its windows which took ten years to build in 1380. The fifteenth-century brass lectern, engraved with the figure of a monk is another treasure.

And Yeovil had its share of excitement in past days. In 1657 the amazing power of a witch's spell was recorded. An old woman gave a magic apple to a young boy, who, regardless of warnings, took a bite and rose in the air flying for three hundred yards! The old woman was tried as a witch and hung at Chard in 1658. Maybe she was a forerunner of the baddie in Snow White!

Many buildings in Yeovil are made of the honey-coloured Ham stone from Handon Hill to the west. There is a museum at Hendford Manor Hall of mainly local history but with a good collection of fire arms.

The most famous museum in the area is at the Royal Naval Air Station at Yeovilton which opened in 1964. This portrays both Naval and Civil aviation from the days of airships and kites, to Concorde and the present day.

At the bottom of Hendford Hill near Yeovil, reached by a waterside walk through woods, are the town's nine springs flowing into a lake.

Muchelney is a small place, once an island in the marshes. There

Left: Glastonbury Thorn: sprigs from the Thorn at St John's Church are sent to the Queen and Queen Mother at Christmas.

'Glastonbury seems timeless.'

Mulcheney Abbey today.

is a toll house, village cross, cedar tree and priest's house. The Benedictines founded an Abbey there in 939 and remains of its church can be seen in the foundations of the Norman abbey church. There is a fifteenth-century Abbot's lodgings with redorter and barn. The wide stairs are much worn, and in the Abbot's room stone lions crouch on pillars twelve feet high each side of the fireplace with a Tudor settle under the window.

Montacute, a masterpiece of an Elizabethan mansion, is four miles west of Yeovil. It is built of Ham Hill stone and, dating from 1598, is one the finest in Britain. The gallery is 189 feet long and runs the length of the second floor with many Elizabethan portraits.

The village is attractive with some buildings dating from the sixteenth century and a Monk's House is fifteenth-century. A priory stood there for over four hundred years until the Dissolution and the gatehouse and some buildings remain.

In the eleventh century St Michael's Hill was known all over England by the discovery of a miracle-working cross. It was moved to Waltham where it cured King Harold's paralysis. 'Holy Cross' was his army's war cry at Hastings. The hill is crowned nowadays with a folly built in 1760.

Barwick, in the neighbourhood, was the home in the nineteenth century of Squire Messiter who built four follies to mark the points of the compass.

Cone folly is seventy-five feet high, a hollow cone with holes like a dovecote tapering to a ball on top. Another has a winged Hermes on a stone. This is known locally as 'Jack the Treacle Eater' representing a young man who carried messages on foot to London

A deserted railway line in an autumn landscape.

and is said to have trained on treacle. Some say he was a milkman's murderer hidden by his wife who fed him on treacle, and he came down from the folly at night to drink. There was a fish tower in the north and an obelisk in the south.

Not content with these four oddities a grotto was also built nearby.

For six hundred years there was a thriving wool industry at Chard until in the nineteenth century local people made the netting from which lace is made.

The highest town in Somerset, it is unusual with a stream running down each side of the street, one flowing into the Bristol Channel and the other into the English Channel. Most of the buildings were destroyed by fire in 1577, the spacious church surviving. Other interesting houses include the Court House where Judge Jeffreys held trial after the Monmouth Rebellion.

One of the most fascinating buildings is the Chough's Hotel dating from 1644. Once said to have been the mansion home of John Stringfellow, the Victorian aviator, it has an unusual history. The name is derived from the red-legged Cornish chough once found in the West of England. A mummified bird, neck outstretched, is kept in a coffin, and superstition claims that nothing must happen to the skeleton. At one time remains of birds were often bricked into chimneys when houses were built and preserved by the lime in the mortar.

After the Monmouth Rebellion Judge Jeffreys stayed at the hotel holding trial at the Court House. His coat of arms was put up in plaster bas relief on the wall of his bedroom and is there to this day. A dozen men were hanged on a large oak tree, known as Hangcross Oak, but it no longer exists.

One landlord of the hotel found a false wall behind a fireplace with a tombstone with the name 'Winifrid' on it — upside down. For some reason it is impossible to photograph the tombstone or the chough. Recently someone tried to take a picture of the bird but nothing came out.

The hotel has a strange history of hidden rooms and a sealed cellar. This may have been an escape tunnel for priests fleeing persecution. And the shadow of a 'nasty old man' by the fireplace could easily have been the dreaded Judge Jeffreys.

Chough's Hotel is obviously a place of intrigue and for centuries has kept its secrets well.

Tractor at work in the Somerset landscape.

The Tudors left their mark on Chard when the clothiers built impressive houses from the profits on wool and cloth sales. Chard School, Manor Court House and Godworthy House and others are still in Fore Street and High Street.

In 1671 William Symes of Poundsford gave his manor to the Burgesses of Chard for conversion to a schoolhouse and Chard School was founded. It was an independent boys' school until 1971 when it became a co-educational preparatory school. The seniors are taught in the Elizabethan buildings of which one is a chapel, and there are also a twentieth-century swimming pool and laboratory.

Famous citizens, apart from John Stringfellow are Sidney Gillingham, a nineteenth-century artificial limb maker, and the town was the birthplace of Margaret Bondfield, the first woman Labour Cabinet Minister.

There is a museum in a sixteenth-century building, originally a farmhouse together with a former inn, which has much of interest relating to the history of Chard from prehistoric times, aspects of social life and relics of both Sidney Gillingham and John Stringfellow. There is also a cider mill and press. Farm implements and vehicles all vividly recreate life in olden days.

Just three miles from Chard is the Ferne Animal Sanctuary established in 1939 to care for hundreds of animals whose owners were called away because of the war. Today, still a charity, over two hundred animals live there from horses to guinea pigs. Over a thousand have been saved from death by the Sanctuary and the work goes on.

Hornsbury Mill was built in the 1860s and is a rural bygones museum with watermill houses of the nineteenth century and even a miller's lavatory!

Cricket St Thomas has an ancient one-thousand-acre estate providing one of the county's leading wildlife parks. The house was made famous in the 'To the Manor Born' television series and was owned by the Hood family, one of whom served with Nelson. The tomb of Alexander Hood in the church has a memory of Lord Nelson in the shape of a memorial to two boys both called Horatio Nelson. It is said that men on the estate carved much of the wooden church furnishings for the fifteenth-century church.

In the wildlife park look out for an unusual tree trunk with an open doorway cut out of it. You can also see llamas, camels, bison, wallabies, flamingoes and other birds, zoo, penguin pool and sheep, cows and goats in a wonderful blend of charm and beauty. It is the home of the National Heavy Horse Centre. A farm and countryside museum has much of interest including a collection of horse-drawn vehicles.

Dating back to Saxon and possibly Roman times the busy small town of Crewkerne is in the south of the county near to Dorset. It was once said that all its streets 'hurried to the market square' maybe due to the Street Fair held at the beginning of September since Saxon times.

The fifteenth-century church has a very striking west front. In the south east corner of the north chapel the oven used for baking the Communion bread dates from the Pre-Reformation days. A small chamber was believed to have been the cell of an anchorite and some claim a hermit lived in the churchyard. William of Orange worshipped here on his way to claim the English throne. There is a tiny Tudor brass of Thomas Golde and two goldsmiths had their inscriptions hammered instead of the normal engraving. Behind the organ lurked a brass of the Martin family showing a monkey looking into a glass. A more macabre memorial to two eighteenth-century children shows a clock pointing to 9.57 — presumably the time of death!

In the nineteenth century sails for the Royal Navy were made here so it is fitting that is should have been the birthplace of two voyagers. William Dampier in the eighteenth century was one of the first Englishmen to set eyes upon Australia and a street is named after him.

Tom Coryate lived a hundred years earlier and walked all over Europe, Greece, Constantinople to Jerusalem, dying of dysentery in India in 1617. He was said to have been the first man to introduce the table fork into England. His worn out shoes hung in Odcombe Church and one is now in a museum.

Captain Hardy was educated at the local Grammar School and sails from here were used in Nelson's ships — maybe even on the *Victory* in which, of course, he served. And those for a modern voyager, Sir Francis Chichester, came from the same town.

At Brympton D'Evercy there is an almost perfect church and a Tudor house of golden hamstone. The sculptured and battlemented front is 130 feet long, and inside is the longest straight staircase in England. There is a collection of watercolours, family wedding

At Brympton D'Evercy there is a Tudor house of golden hamstone.

dresses and other items on show. The tiny dower house has a turret, and the church has a bellcote like a lantern, with tombs of the D'Evercys showing one thirteenth-century lady, her puppies at her feet. There is the tomb of John Sydenham with a canopy of his arms and a skeleton in stone underneath with three skulls and a curious epitaph. There is also a sensitive effigy of a priest said to have been seized by the Black Death while saying Mass in 1346.

Hinton St George is a lovely village with old houses and another beautiful church. The home of the Pauletts since the fifteenth century, it has many reminders of the family. There is a medieval village cross with a figure of John the Baptist on its shaft and it is still standing. The church is fifteenth-century and some five hundred years ago someone chiselled the daggers of the Pauletts and the cross of St George on the font made by the Normans three hundred years earlier. Some brasses of the fifteenth century were returned to the church from one in Warwickshire in 1948. The Paulett memorials dating from 1475 to 1962 are of much interest, and there is one to Sir Amyas Paulett, gaoler to Mary, Queen of Scots. The title became extinct in 1973.

The Duke of Monmouth was said to cure Elizabeth Parcet of

scrofula when she touched him while he was on a tour of the county, demonstrating to some that he was the rightful king with the power to cure the 'king's evil'.

In October the village is the scene of the Punkie Night festival which is still observed with the villagers bearing lanterns and singing through the streets.

Wincanton is of architectural and archaeological interest and now well-known for horse racing, for it is one of the twenty-four racecourses in England devoted entirely to jumping, out of the fifty-nine in the country. It is also one of the racecourses owned by the Racing Trust, a subsidiary of the Jockey Club, and the sport of steeplechasing grew from the country sport of riding to hounds. It began as a race from one village church steeple to another — hence the name. Hurdles are usually about three feet six inches in height and horses progress from hurdle racing to the more formidable fences in the steeplechase course. One of the jockeys often seen at Wincanton is John Francome who, so far, has ridden more winners than any other 'jump' jockey.

The town was the traditional remounting point for the Royal Mail and other coaches since the eighteenth century. The coaching inns remain and the connection with horses has long been a feature.

In the churchyard is an effigy of note erected by Nathaniel Ireson to himself! He was a potter and builder and the base shows the tools of his trade. He added a chancel to the church which has a carved stone, maybe medieval, built into the wall of the porch showing St Aloys the blacksmith who became a bishop. He is at an anvil, the leg of a horse in his hand, while the horse waits patiently. The bishop, horse and an attendant are all headless.

North Cadbury has a fifteenth-century church with beam ends in the south aisle showing a Tudor cat and mousetrap, believed to be the only one in existence. Another shows two dragons hatching from eggs and a windmill. One is dated 1538.

South Cadbury Castle is a natural hill fort much favoured by the Early Britons and Romans whose coins have been found there. This fort covering eighteen acres was of importance, and is also one of the legendary Camelots of King Arthur with Arthur's Well, St Anne's Wishing Well, a Palace and Arthur's hunting path to Glastonbury. It is a wonderful place from which to view the county.

The Augustinian Abbey at Bruton has long since gone but part of the wall and the dovecote, set in a meadow on a hill, remains. It is tower-like, stone-built with mullioned window and four gables, probably dating from the early sixteenth century.

There is a packhorse bridge called Little Bow and King's, a famous school founded in 1519, is where R. D. Blackmore discovered a copy of Magna Carta. The old town was a Royal Borough created by Saxon Kings and even had a mint. The church has two towers one shorter than the other. Sexey's Hospital was built in the seventeenth century by Hugh Sexey, Auditor of Exchequer to Queen Elizabeth I.

There are ten remaining lockups in Somerset, and probably the most famous is the domed one at Castle Cary. This is called the Pepper Pot and was built in 1779 at a cost of £23, and is one of only four similar in Britain. It was used at one time to imprison children caught playing games on Sunday!

The town also boasts the only horse hair machine in the country. The former Dolphin Inn — now selling antiques — had a high window where the ostlers' boy watched for the coaches coming along the road and warned the ostlers to get the horses ready.

One curious feature of this old market town is the raised pavements at each end known locally as batches, rising to six or seven feet. The war memorial cross stood on an island in the horsepond.

Lodge Hill where a castle once stood affords wonderful views.

Templecombe is named after the Knights Templar who founded a preceptory there in the twelfth century and remains of the building can be seen at the manor house.

The church was founded by a daughter of Alfred and it has a long, long history and a Norman font. A picture of Christ on the wall, faded and on rough wood is most strangely preserved. In 1951 a gale damaged a cottage, once the priest's cottage, and revealed a panel in the roof which proved to be a life-size medieval head of Christ, said to be similar to that of the image on the Turin Shroud. This revealed a secret kept for hundreds of years. It is thought the Templars obtained the shroud on a crusade and brought it back to this country. One of the barns in which they were believed to have eaten is still standing.

The Templars Order was suppressed in the fourteenth century and one reason given was that they worshipped Christ without a halo. Behind the manor farm is a building believed to have been the Preceptory Chapel.

Left: The Caratacus Stone on Exmoor.
Above: An unusual angle of Dunster.

Also Available

LEGENDS OF SOMERSET
by Sally Jones. 65 photographs and drawings.
Sally Jones travels across rich legendary landscapes. Words, drawings and photographs all combine to evoke a spirit of adventure.
'On the misty lands of the Somerset Plain – as Sally Jones makes clear – history, legend and fantasy are inextricably mixed.'

Dan Lees, The Western Daily Press

STRANGE SOMERSET STORIES
Introduced by David Foot with chapters by Ray Waddon, Jack Hurley, Lornie Leete-Hodge, Hilary Wreford, David Foot, Rosemary Clinch and Michael Williams.
' . . . a good collection of yarns about Somerset's eccentrics, weird legends and architectural follies . . .'

Dan Lees, The Western Daily Press

SOMERSET IN THE OLD DAYS
by David Young. 145 old photographs.
David Young of TSW takes a journey in words and old pictures across Somerset.
'Illustrated by a charm-filled collection of old photographs, David Young's book fairly reeks of nostalgia.' The Western Morning News

EXMOOR IN THE OLD DAYS
by Rosemary Anne Lauder. 147 photographs.
The author perceptively shows that Exmoor is not only the most beautiful of our Westcountry moors but is also rich in history and character: a world of its own in fact.
'. . . contains scores of old photographs and picture postcards . . . will provide a passport for many trips down memory lane . . .'

Bideford Gazette

CURIOSITIES OF DEVON
by Michael Williams.
Michael Williams explores strange and unusual aspects of a county of contrasts; curious customs and characters, strange architecture and landscapes, and highly individual Dartmoor characters. There are visits to the Finch Foundry at Sticklepath and Arlington Court.

CURIOSITIES OF CORNWALL
by Michael Williams. 62 photographs.
Eccentric architecture; customs — curious, Cornish and Royal; curious characters and a curiosity that grew into invention and innovation; the deep hole at Delabole; the question witch or saint? . . . all these and much more prove that Cornwall has more than her share of curiosities.
'. . . *a fascinating new book . . . avid collectors of offbeat gems of knowledge, whether they belong to the county or not, will welcome it as a treasure . . .*'
Pamela Leeds, The Western Evening Herald

AROUND GLORIOUS DEVON
by David Young. 148 photographs.
David Young, well known in the Westcountry as TSW's roving architect, takes us on a personally-conducted tour of his glorious Devon.
'. . . *proves as good a guide in print as he is on the small screen.*'
Judy Diss, Herald Express

VIEWS OF OLD PLYMOUTH
by Sarah Foot.
Words and old pictures combine to recall Plymouth as it once was: a reminder of those great times past and of the spirit of the people of Plymouth.
'*This is a lovely nostalgia-ridden book and one which no real Plymothian will want to be without.*'
James Mildren, The Western Morning News

VIEWS OF OLD DEVON
Rosemary Anne Lauder provides the text for more than 200 old postcards, evocative of a world and a way of life that has gone. Words and pictures combine to produce a book that will delight all who love Devon.
'*Only the camera can turn back the clock like this.*'
The Sunday Independent

MOUNT'S BAY
by Douglas Williams.
More than 120 old photographs of an area stretching from Land's End to the Lizard with perceptive text by one of Cornwall's most respected journalists.
'. . . *a fascinating and exhaustive study . . . It is a guidebook, potted history, pictorial gallery of Cornish life – all these things and very much more.*'
The Western Evening Herald

GHOSTS OF DEVON
by Peter Underwood. 44 photographs and drawings.
Peter Underwood, President of the Ghost Club, writes of the ghostly stories that saturate the County of Devon, a land full of mystery and of ghostly lore and legend.
'Packed with photographs, this is a fascinating book.' Herald Express

SUPERSTITION AND FOLKLORE
by Michael Williams. 44 photographs.
A survey of Westcountry Superstitions: interviews on the subject and some Cornish and Devon folklore.
'. . . the strictures that we all ignore at our peril. To help us to keep out of trouble, Mr Williams has prepared a comprehensive list.'
Frank Kempe, North Devon Journal-Herald

SEA STORIES OF DEVON
In this companion volume to *Sea Stories of Cornwall* nine Westcountry authors recall stirring events and people from Devon's sea past. Well illustrated with old and new photographs, it is introduced by best-selling novelist E. V. Thompson.
'The tales themselves are interesting and varied but the real strength of the book lies in the wealth of illustration, with photographs and pictures on practically every page.' Jane Leigh, Express & Echo

NORTH CORNWALL IN THE OLD DAYS
by Joan Rendell. 147 old photographs.
These pictures and Joan Rendell's perceptive text combine to give us many facets of a nostalgic way of North Cornish life, stretching from Newquay to the Cornwall/Devon border.
'This remarkable collection of pictures is a testimony to a people, a brave and uncomplaining race.' Pamela Leeds, The Western Evening Herald

STRANGE STORIES FROM DEVON
by Rosemary Anne Lauder and Michael Williams. 46 photographs.
Strange shapes and places — strange characters — the man they couldn't hang, and a Salcombe mystery, the Lynmouth disaster and a mysterious house are only some of the strange stories.
'A riveting read'. The Plymouth Times
'. . . well-written and carefully edited.'
Monica Wyatt, Teignmouth Post & Gazette

We shall be pleased to send you our catalogue giving full details of our growing list of titles for Devon, Cornwall and Somerset and forthcoming publications.

If you have difficulty in obtaining our titles, write direct to Bossiney Books, Land's End, St Teath, Bodmin, Cornwall.